ACHIEVE LEVEL 5
ENGLISH

By **Sheila Hentall** and **Helen Ward**

Rising Stars UK Ltd, 76 Farnaby Road, Bromley, BR1 4BH
Website: www.risingstars-uk.com

Every effort has been made to trace copyright holders and obtain their permission for the use of copyright material. The authors and publishers will gladly receive information enabling them to rectify any error or omission in subsequent editions.

All facts are correct at time of going to press.

Published 2002
New Edition
Text, design and layout © Rising Stars UK Ltd.

Editorial: Tanya Solomons
Design and Artwork: Marc Burville-Riley, Claire Harvey
Cover photo: copyright © GETTY IMAGES/Dana Edmunds

Acknowledgements
Anne Fine, "Chat Show Chicken" from *The Chicken Gave It To Me*
© Anne Fine 1992. First published by Egmont Books Ltd, London,
and used with permission.

Compassion in World Farming Ltd. www.ciwf.co.uk <http://www.ciwf.co.uk/>

All rights reserved. No part of this publication may be reproduced, stored in a retrieval system, or transmitted, in any form by any means, electronic, mechanical, photocopying, recording or otherwise, without the prior permission of Rising Stars.

British Library Cataloguing in Publication Data
A CIP record for this book is available from the British Library.

ISBN: 0-9542202-0-X

Printed in Grimsby, UK

Contents

How to use this book	4
Section 1: Writing Non-fiction	6
Section 2: Writing Fiction	24
Section 3: Reading Comprehension	34
Section 4: Grammar	40
Section 5: Vocabulary	48
Section 6: Spelling	52
Section 7: Punctuation	56
Section 8: Handwriting	59
Test Technique	60
The 2003 SATs	62
Index	64

How to use this book

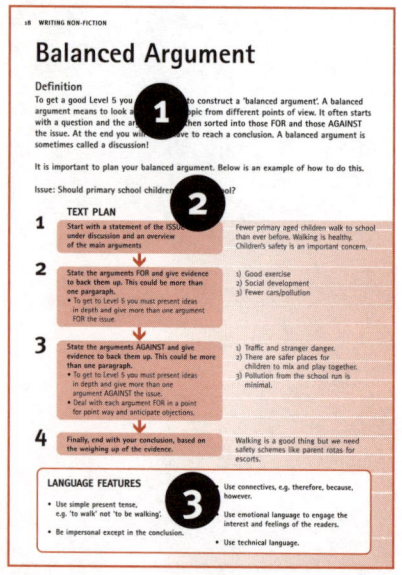 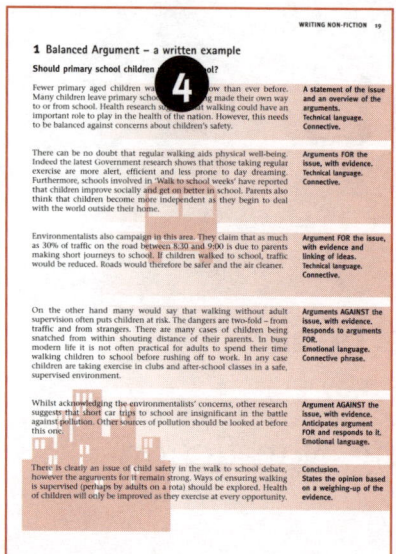 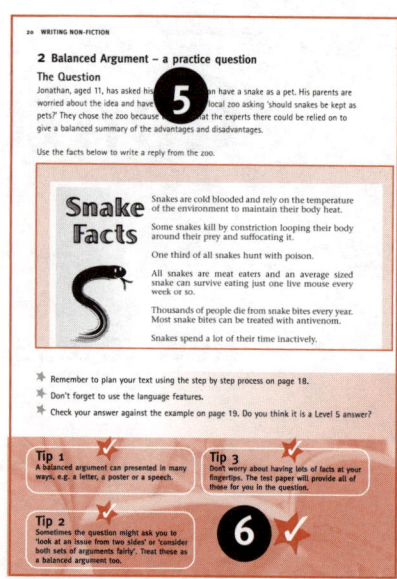

WRITING FICTION AND NON-FICTION

① Definition – This explains the topic simply and explains why it is important.

② Text Plan – Each type of writing is explained in a step by step format to help you plan. Planning is very important when writing fiction and non-fiction and these charts will help you plan properly.

③ Language Features – These are useful. They summarise the main characteristics of each type of text.

④ The Written Example – This gives you an example of a well-written piece of text which follows the Text Plan and contains the Language Features. Notes in the margin highlight the key points for you.

⑤ Practice Question – This is where you do the work! Try answering the questions by using the Text Plan and by referring to the Language Features. Compare it against the written example - is your answer good enough for a Level 5?

⑥ Tips – These give you helpful hints and general tips that are well worth remembering!

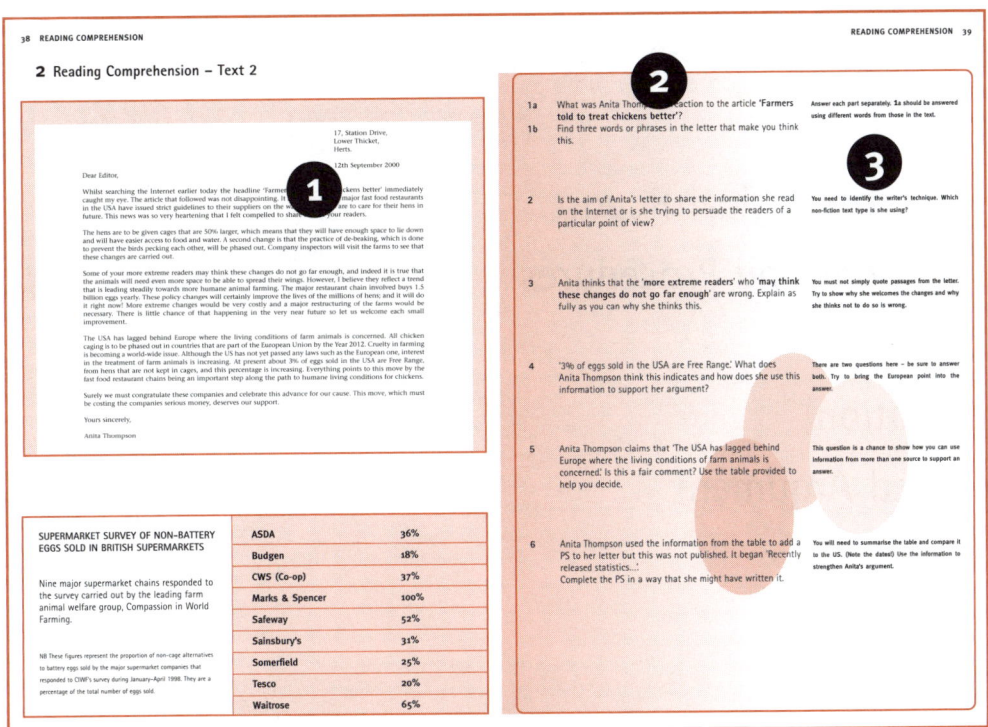

READING COMPREHENSION

❶ Text Example – This gives you a typical example of a piece of text that you might find in your SATs test.

❷ Questions – The text is followed by a number of questions relating to the text. These are typical examples of 2 and 3 mark questions, which you need to be able to answer to get to Level 5.

❸ Guidance Notes – These notes are there to help you write an answer that will give you full marks!

In addition you will find over 100 clear tips and facts to help you with

★ Grammar ★ Spelling ★ Punctuation ★ Vocabulary ★ Handwriting

If you use this guidance to help you prepare for your test, you will have a great chance of getting to Level 5!

WRITING NON-FICTION

In this section we are looking at the six main types of non-fiction writing. These are:

- ✦ Non-chronological Report
- ✦ Instructions and Procedures
- ✦ Recount
- ✦ Explanation
- ✦ Balanced Argument
- ✦ Persuasion

Each type of non-fiction writing has been broken down so that you can focus on the distinguishing features of each text type.

- The **definition** gives you a summary of the role of that type of writing.

- The **language features** describe the main characteristics of the text type.

- The **text organisation** tells you exactly how to set out your work.

- The **text example** gives you an idea of what the type looks like in a finished form. It is annotated to help you identify the language features.

So what do I need to do now?

- Study and work through each type of non-fiction writing.

- Note the different text types and their characteristics.

- Complete the practice question at the end of each section.

When completing the practice question

- Take your time planning and checking, as well as writing.

- Check your work against the checklist of 'language features' and go back to alter and improve your work if necessary. (Remember, it can be easy to forget your time connectives.)

- If you check and improve your work by adding in language features, your work will improve significantly and you will achieve more marks!

- Remember that from 2003 you will be marked on your handwriting in each of the Writing Tests so try to keep it neat!

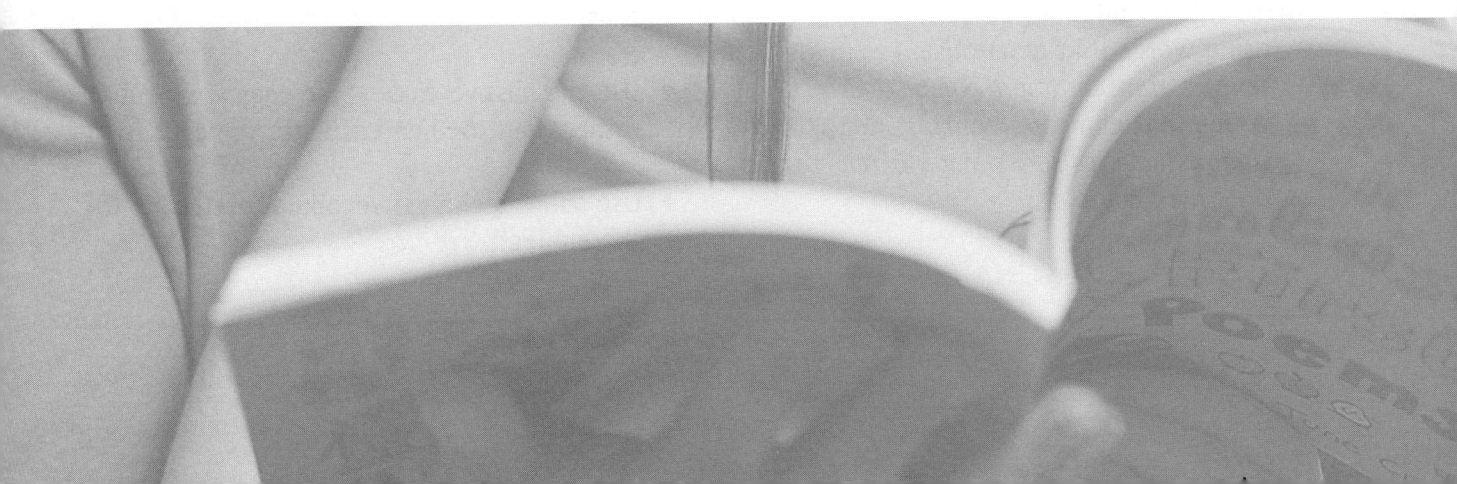

Non-chronological Report

Definition
A report presents factual information in a clear and systematic way. The precise structure will depend on the subject and will be driven by the purpose of the report, which is **to describe things the way they are**. Diagrams or tables often support this form of writing.

Topic: Volcanoes

TEXT PLAN

1 Introduce the topic with a definition and follow this up with more technical classification. Make it clear what the report will be about.

Level 5 writers will use correct generic terms (group names).
Lava erupting at weakness in crust. Define lava and magma.

2 Give a description of the subject by some of its qualities or uses.

What causes an eruption? What are craters and vents?

3 Follow with a number of paragraphs each presenting detailed information on different aspects of the topic.

These paragraphs should be presented in a logical order. Level 5 writers must elaborate on the more important points.
Volcanoes changing the earth. Volcanoes on the seabed.

4 Return to some of the main points as an ending comment.

Volcanoes still change the earth.

LANGUAGE FEATURES

- Use vocabulary choices that are factual and precise – descriptive but not imaginative. These will include:
  - using words that generalise, such as *reptiles, transportation, humankind.*
  - words that compare, contrast and classify, such as *identical, are similar to, related, are classified as.*

- Write in a formal style, so do not use the pronouns 'I' or 'we' or give opinions.

- Write in the simple – timeless – present tense.

- Use the passive voice – *the eggs are incubated* rather than *the hen incubates the eggs.*

- Use some technical vocabulary relevant to the subject.

1 Non-chronological Report – a written example

Volcanoes – still shaping the earth

A volcano is a land form that is created by an opening in the Earth's surface spewing out hot liquid rock from inside the Earth's mantle. This liquid rock, called magma, forces its way through weak spots in the Earth's crust and pours out as hot lava.	**Definition and classification. Complex sentence giving further technical information. Technical vocabulary.**
When magma reaches the Earth's surface it flows out through an opening called a vent. As lava flows out it cools quickly and becomes solid rock around the vent. The opening at the top of a volcano's vent is the crater. If the vent has been plugged by lava from previous eruptions, pressure can build up within the volcano and become so great that the lava blasts its way to the surface. Volcanic eruptions are often violent explosions and spectacular outpourings of fiery molten rocks.	**Powerful 'action' verbs create a precise description. Descriptive but not imaginary language.**
Volcanoes have played an important part in shaping the Earth's surface. Most of the volcanoes on Earth are not currently active, but there are still more than 600 that are. The Hawaiian volcano Kilauea, that has been erupting continuously since January 3, 1983, illustrates how the world is still being shaped by volcanoes. Another recent example is the eruption of Mayon, in the Philippines, in 1984. The lava flows from this volcano caused 73,000 people to leave their homes!	**Examples support the subject of this paragraph. Connecting phrase links the two points.**
Volcanoes can form on the sea bed where they are capable of creating and destroying whole islands. Indeed there are more volcanoes under the sea than on land. In 1963 a new island suddenly appeared in the sea off Iceland. It was the tip of a volcano that stood on the ocean floor. For three years the volcano was active. The lava cooled to form Surtsey, which is now an island about 1.5 kilometres in diameter. In contrast the volcanic eruption of 1883, on Krakatoa, destroyed the entire island.	**Elaborating on the first point in the sentence with an example. Past tense. Language of comparison.**
Television has made it possible for pictures of the volcanoes spewing up fire and rocks to be seen around the world. However, humankind is still at the mercy of volcanoes. Scientists can never be sure when another volcano may erupt, so Surtsey may not remain the newest island on Earth for long.	**Use of a formal generic term 'humankind' rather than 'we'.**

2 Non-chronological Report – a practice question

The Question

Prepare and write a report entitled **'THE FASTEST ANIMALS – how would humans feature?'**

Here are some facts about the speeds at which different animals can travel.

THE WORLD'S FASTEST AND SLOWEST ANIMALS

On the African savannah three kinds of hunting techniques are used by predators:

1. **Ambushing** – sneaking up on prey which is taken by surprise and then pursuing it if necessary.
2. **Working as a pack** – persistence and sheer numbers of the hunters mean that the prey cannot escape.
3. **Outrunning** – sprinting over short distances to bring down the prey.

- The cheetah is the world's fastest land animal. They can sprint at over 100 km/h when hunting but tire very quickly. The cheetah is built for speed with:
  – exceptionally long legs allowing it to take huge strides.
  – ridged foot pads, which provide traction, rather like a car's tyre.
  – a streamlined body and small head offering very little wind resistance.
  – a flexible spine rather like a giant spring.
- The three-toed sloth is the slowest mammal, taking a whole day to travel about 100 metres. American naturalist William Beebe once followed a sloth for a week in the forest. He said it spent 10 hours resting, 11 hours feeding, 18 hours moving slowly, and 129 hours sleeping! Answering a distress call from her baby, a mother sloth has been seen to sprint 4 m/min.
- Swifts are perfectly adapted for high speed flight, with a streamlined body and scythe-like wings. The tail is short and forked.
- The peregrine falcon is a bird of prey. It is lightning fast as it swoops (dives) down on smaller birds in flight, sometimes reaching 180 km/h.

Speed facts (kilometres per hour)

CREATURE	spine-tailed swift	sailfish	cheetah	racing pigeon	gazelle	shark	zebra	ostrich	lion	giraffe	human	sloth	snail
SPEED	160+	110	100+	97+	80+	64	64	64	58	51	32	0.1	0.05

⭐ Text plan – brainstorm the facts and use a spider diagram.

⭐ Organise the facts into a logical paragraph plan. (Use the step by step text plan on page 8.) Note how the theme of each paragraph will be elaborated and think of examples that support these points.

⭐ When your report is written, check it against the text and language features at the start of this section. Is the answer a Level 5 answer?

Tip 1
Watch out for reports that ask for an **evaluation**. These should still be formal but will need to be written in the first person using 'I' or 'we'.

Tip 2
Sometimes newspaper articles are called reports. Be careful! These have different rules. (See the Recount section on page 13.)

Instructions and Procedures

Definition

Instructions and procedures tell you how something is done. You need to use a step by step approach, with organised sentences instructing your reader. To achieve Level 5, writers need to:

 always use detailed, precise adverbs and adjectives to assist the reader.

 be able to use different framework headings according to the subject, while using the same overall structure.

TEXT PLAN

1	Goal – a statement of what needs to be done.	For example 'How to make a model ship'.
2	A list of the materials and equipment needed. List them in the order in which they are required.	You might present this information in numbered points, a table or in several clearly organised paragraphs using headings and sub-headings.
3	A step by step account of the method used to achieve the goal.	You might use well-labelled diagrams to clarify instructions.
4	Sometimes an evaluation or conclusion is appropriate.	

LANGUAGE FEATURES

- Write in the simple present tense, e.g. you mix, you cut, you shake.
- Use an imperative or bossy tone, e.g. Mix the flour then stir for 5 minutes.
- Write in chronological order using time connectives, e.g. first, then, next, when.
- Use mainly action verbs, e.g. mix, put, roll.
- Include detailed factual information, e.g. shape, size, colour, amount.
- Include information about how, where and when.
- Generalise participants and readers. Don't write about named individuals or people.

Tip

Instructions and Procedures can be presented in many different ways:
- recipes
- instructions for a game
- science experiments
- machinery manuals

The overall structure is the same for each one but the headings are different - TAKE CARE!

1 Instructions and Procedures – a written example

How to make a chocolate sponge cake

INGREDIENTS			
For the cake		**For the filling**	Clear organisation with sub-headings.
175 g margarine	pinch of salt	Jam or	
175 g caster sugar	1 tsp baking powder	Chocolate spread	
150 g self-raising flour	5 tbsp cocoa powder		
	3 eggs		

Method

1. Preheat oven to 180°C/350°F/gas mark 4. *Numbered points for clarity.*
2. Grease two 20 cm sandwich tins and line with greaseproof paper. *Imperative (bossy) verb*
3. Cream margarine and sugar in large bowl.
4. Sift flour, salt, baking powder and cocoa into the bowl.
5. Add the eggs and mix carefully until the mixture is smooth.
6. Divide the mixture evenly between the tins. *Action verb.*
7. Bake for 20–25 minutes until the cakes are springy to the touch and have left the edges of the tin. *Adjective to assist reader*
8. Remove cakes from oven and allow to cool in tins for about 5 minutes. Turn out carefully onto cooling rack. *Adverb to assist reader*
9. When cool, spread jam or chocolate spread on one cake and sandwich the other on top.

2 Instructions and Procedures – a practice question

The Question

Imagine you have an elderly aunt coming to stay. She is very independent and has insisted on finding her own way to your house. She says that all she needs is a clear set of instructions and perhaps a map to direct her to your home from the nearest station. Your writing task is to write her a letter, which contains all the necessary information.

★ Plan your text using the step by step instructions on page 11.

★ Write your letter then check it carefully to make sure you have used all the language features that you need.

★ Re-read your work. Would a stranger be able to find your home?

Recount

Definition
A recount retells events – telling it like it is or was.
There are different types of recounts:
- Retelling a personal experience
- Retelling a factual event or incident
- Relating an imaginary event (this will call upon narrative writing skills)

A recount can include the writer's personal interpretation of events.

To achieve Level 5, writers need to:

★ elaborate on important events and leave out insignificant details.

★ include relevant detail and description to engage the reader.

★ vary sentence beginnings to make the recount more interesting.

TEXT PLAN

1 Orientation – this is information that helps the reader understand the recount (who, where, when, why).

- **Who?** Us; other drivers.
- **Where?** Traffic lights on Dartmouth Road.
- **When?** Saturday morning.
- **Why?** Snow and icy conditions.
- **What?** Two cars collided; one hit lamppost.

2 Recount events in chronological order (as they happened) making sure the event is broken down clearly.

- **Event 1** Driving along in snow looking at Christmas lights. Roads icy.
- **Event 2** Dad shouts, hits icy patch, loses control, hits car in front.
- **Event 3** Car pushed across road into path of oncoming vehicle.

3 Give some personal comment or reflection about the event.

Dad driving too fast and not concentrating; council hadn't put grit on the road.

4 Sum up by returning to some of the main points as an ending comment. Some evaluation may be appropriate.

It was a shame – cast a shadow over Christmas.

LANGUAGE FEATURES

- Write in the past tense but personal response/comments will involve moving into the present tense.

- Write in chronological order.

- Use time connectives to sustain the chronological order, e.g. next, then, after, meanwhile, subsequently.

- Write in a personal tone, using I, we, he, she and they.

- Use powerful verbs.

1 Recount – a written example

An eyewitness account of the car crash

On Saturday morning we were driving along Dartmouth Road to pick up some last minute Christmas presents. The weather was appalling – Friday's snow had settled and hardened, leaving large icy patches on the road. Snow had started falling again and we were admiring the effect of the Christmas lights through the snowflakes.	Who, where, when and why presented in three sentences. Details significant to the recount elaborated on. Final sentence anticipates the accident by mentioning their attention being on the Christmas lights. Leading into the next paragraph.
Then the snow started to fall more heavily; it was looking rather like a Christmas card. Dad was enjoying the view and didn't notice the lights turn to red.	Details and description included to add interest.
Just at that moment, we hit a particularly icy patch. Dad shouted out, "I'm losing control!" The car careered forward and smashed into the car in front. It was terrifying; for a second or two we had no idea how we were ever going to come to a stop. We were all flung forward as Dad tried to regain control of the car.	Powerful verbs. Past tense.
Within seconds the force of the impact had pushed the car in front across the road and right into the path of an oncoming vehicle. Fortunately, the driver was paying more attention than my Dad and he was able to swing out of the way. Unfortunately, he did collide with a lamppost.	Variety of sentence structures and sentence beginnings to maintain the reader's interest. The writer's personal interpretation of events.
Although no one was physically hurt, everyone in the cars involved was badly shaken. There was also a lot of damage to three cars and a lamppost. It may sound disloyal to say this, but I think my Dad was to blame. However, had the council gritted the road on Friday night, perhaps the icy patch would not have been there in the first place!	Past tense but personal comments move into present tense.
Unfortunately, a short lapse in concentration caused a shadow to be cast over Christmas. What a pity.	Concluding sentence evaluates the event.

WRITING NON-FICTION 15

2 Recount – a practice question

Here is some information about Guy Fawkes:

- Guy Fawkes was a member of a secret group that wanted to get rid of King James I because he wasn't a Catholic.
- Guy Fawkes rented a cellar underneath the Houses of Parliament and hid barrels of gunpowder there.
- The plan was to blow up the Houses of Parliament on 5th November 1605.
- One of the members of the group boasted about the idea to a friend and the King's guards found out.
- The conspirators were caught just as they were about to light the fuse. They were arrested and subsequently executed.

The Question

Writing as if you were one of the group with Guy Fawkes, write your diary entry recounting these events.

⭐ Start with a text plan

Who?	Where?	When?	Why?	What?
Event 1	Event 2	Event 3	Reflection	Ending summary

⭐ Sort this plan into paragraphs using the step by step plan on page 13. It may be helpful to identify some time connectives.

⭐ When your recount is written, check it against the step by step text plan and language features on page 13.

⭐ Is your answer a Level 5 answer?

Tip

Recounts can be presented in many different ways:
- biographies
- autobiographies
- newspaper reports of events
- diaries, histories, letters
- other eyewitness accounts of incidents

They are sometimes referred to as reports but remember, a chronological report should be written as a recount!

Explanation

Definition
An explanation explains how something works, e.g. how a car works, or why things are the way they are, e.g. why some animals hibernate. It gives a full account of the processes involved. Some explanations cover how and why.

TEXT PLAN

1 Start with a clear and precise definition of the phenomena. Use the simple present tense.

Most animals grow two sets of teeth.

2 Describe the parts.

What is it? Be clear and only use information you understand.
Number of teeth. Types of teeth.

3 Describe the operation in a step by step, logical way.

How and why it works, using action verbs to explain the process.

4 Explain where and when it is used.

Use connectives and show cause and effect.
Importance of oral hygiene.

5 You may need to add information about special features. Then finish with a summing up paragraph which completes the explanation. Evaluation may be appropriate.

Include special features and then sum up. It may be appropriate to give an evaluation.

To achieve Level 5, writers need to:

- use specific vocabulary and technical terms. Definitions may be required.
- maintain a clear and logical approach. The cause and effect relationship is very important and connectives must show this.

LANGUAGE FEATURES

- Write in the simple present tense, e.g. Animals often hibernate.
- Use connectives that reflect passing time, e.g. then, later, finally.
- Use mostly action verbs to describe processes, e.g. cuts, tears, grinds.
- Show cause and effect clearly, e.g. consequently, as a result of, so, then.
- Generalise non-human participants, e.g. the rain, mountains, electricity.

1 Explanation – a written example

How do teeth work?

Most animals, including humans, grow two sets of teeth in a lifetime. The first set is called the milk teeth; the second is the permanent teeth. Teeth are used for cutting, tearing and grinding food. There are 20 milk teeth in a child's jaw and 32 in a full adult set. Each jaw has 4 biting teeth [incisors], 2 tearing and holding teeth [canines], 4 chewing and cutting teeth [bicuspids] and 6 grinding teeth [molars]. Teeth are made up of 3 parts: the crown [covered by hard enamel], the neck and the root [which holds the tooth in the jaw]. Underneath the hard enamel, the tooth is composed of dentine, which is a softer substance.

Simple present tense.
Technical language.

Description of 'how teeth work'.

Action verbs.

Teeth need to be looked after. Tooth decay damages strong teeth, causing pain and restricting their use. Tooth decay is caused when pieces of food left between the teeth become acidic and attack the enamel. Bacteria in the mouth speed up this process. Consequently, oral hygiene is very important – teeth should be carefully brushed at least twice a day to ensure no food particles remain around them. Regular visits to the dentist can also prevent small holes in the enamel remaining unnoticed and becoming larger. Dentists monitor the condition of teeth and will block holes with fillings. Serious tooth decay can lead to the removal of some or all the teeth. In these cases, false teeth have to be fitted instead.

Cause and effect.

Connectives.

Action verbs.

2 Explanation – a practice question

Write an explanation of **'How libraries work'** using the following information to help you. Add more information if you can find it in a non-fiction book or encyclopaedia but don't copy or include information you don't understand!

How do libraries work?
- Libraries hold stocks of books for the public to borrow or refer to.
- Non-fiction and fiction books are available.
- To take out a book, a membership card or ticket is needed.
- Most libraries have computerised systems, which are used for loaning stock and locating particular books from other libraries in the area.
- Libraries have special sections for young children, teenagers and adults.
- Many loan out music and videos.
- Access to the Internet and photocopying facilities are available.
- Community groups and book-related activities happen throughout the week.

★ Plan your text using the steps on page 16.

★ When you have completed your explanation check it includes the language features – is it a Level 5 answer?

Balanced Argument

Definition

To get a good Level 5 you must be able to construct a 'balanced argument'. A balanced argument means to look at an issue or topic from different points of view. It often starts with a question and the arguments are then sorted into those FOR and those AGAINST the issue. At the end you will often have to reach a conclusion. A balanced argument is sometimes called a discussion!

It is important to plan your balanced argument. Below is an example of how to do this.

Issue: Should primary school children walk to school?

TEXT PLAN

1 Start with a statement of the ISSUE under discussion and an overview of the main arguments.

Fewer primary aged children walk to school than ever before. Walking is healthy. Children's safety is an important concern.

2 State the arguments FOR and give evidence to back them up. This could be more than one paragraph.
- To get to Level 5 you must present ideas in depth and give more than one argument FOR the issue.

1) Good exercise
2) Social development
3) Fewer cars/pollution

3 State the arguments AGAINST and give evidence to back them up. This could be more than one paragraph.
- To get to Level 5 you must present ideas in depth and give more than one argument AGAINST the issue.
- Deal with each argument FOR in a point for point way and anticipate objections.

1) Traffic and stranger danger.
2) There are safer places for children to mix and play together.
3) Pollution from the school run is minimal.

4 Finally, end with your conclusion, based on the weighing-up of the evidence.

Walking is a good thing but we need safety schemes like parent rotas for escorts.

LANGUAGE FEATURES

- Use simple present tense, e.g. 'to walk' not 'to be walking'.
- Be impersonal except in the conclusion.
- Use connectives, e.g. therefore, because, however.
- Use emotional language to engage the interest and feelings of the readers.
- Use technical language.

1 Balanced Argument – a written example

Should primary school children walk to school?

Fewer primary aged children walk to school now than ever before. Many children leave primary school never having made their own way to or from school. Health research suggests that walking could have an important role to play in the health of the nation. However, this needs to be balanced against concerns about children's safety.	A statement of the issue and an overview of the arguments. Technical language. Connective.
There can be no doubt that regular walking aids physical well-being. Indeed the latest Government research shows that those taking regular exercise are more alert, efficient and less prone to daydreaming. Furthermore, schools involved in 'Walk to school weeks' have reported that children improve socially and get on better in school. Parents also think that children become more independent as they begin to deal with the world outside their home.	Arguments FOR the issue, with evidence. Technical language. Connective.
Environmentalists also campaign in this area. They claim that as much as 30% of traffic on the road between 8:30 and 9:00 is due to parents making short journeys to school. If children walked to school, traffic would be reduced. Roads would therefore be safer and the air cleaner.	Argument FOR the issue, with evidence and linking of ideas. Technical language. Connective.
On the other hand many would say that walking without adult supervision often puts children at risk. The dangers are two-fold – from traffic and from strangers. There are many cases of children being snatched from within shouting distance of their parents. In busy modern life it is not often practical for adults to spend their time walking children to school before rushing off to work. In any case children are taking exercise in clubs and after-school classes in a safe, supervised environment.	Arguments AGAINST the issue, with evidence. Responds to arguments FOR. Emotional language. Connective phrase.
While acknowledging the environmentalists' concerns, other research suggests that short car trips to school are insignificant in the battle against pollution. Other sources of pollution should be looked at before this one.	Argument AGAINST the issue, with evidence. Anticipates argument FOR and responds to it. Emotional language.
There is clearly an issue of child safety in the walk to school debate, however the arguments for it remain strong. Ways of ensuring walking is supervised (perhaps by adults on a rota) should be explored. The health of children will only be improved if they exercise at every opportunity.	Conclusion. States the opinion based on a weighing-up of the evidence.

2 Balanced Argument – a practice question

The Question

Jonathan, aged 11, has asked his parents if he can have a snake as a pet. His parents are worried about the idea and have written to the local zoo asking 'should snakes be kept as pets?' They chose the zoo because they felt that the experts there could be relied on to give a balanced summary of the advantages and disadvantages.

Use the facts below to write a reply from the zoo.

Snakes are cold-blooded and rely on the temperature of the environment to maintain their body heat.

Some snakes kill by constriction, looping their body around their prey and suffocating it.

One third of all snakes hunt with poison.

All snakes are meat eaters and an average sized snake can survive eating just one live mouse every week or so.

Thousands of people die from snake bites every year. Most snake bites can be treated with anti-venom.

Snakes spend a lot of their time inactively.

★ Remember to plan your text using the step by step process on page 18.

★ Don't forget to use the language features.

★ Check your answer against the example on page 19. Do you think it is a Level 5 answer?

Tip 1
A balanced argument can be presented in many ways, e.g. a letter, a poster or a speech.

Tip 3
Don't worry about having lots of facts at your fingertips. The test paper will provide all of those for you in the question.

Tip 2
Sometimes the question might ask you to 'look at an issue from two sides' or 'consider both sets of arguments fairly'. Treat these as a balanced argument too.

Persuasion

Definition
To write a persuasive argument is to develop a logical argument from a particular point of view in order to persuade others. It often starts with a question. Ideas are developed and supporting details added in order to give a logical and convincing presentation of the case. The writer chooses either:

(a) to argue persuasively from one point of view

or

(b) to appear to give a balanced argument but, by carefully selecting and logically presenting the information, leads the reader to the writer's point of view.

TEXT PLAN

1 Start with a clear presentation of the point to be argued followed by a summary of the main arguments.

The argument must not be presented as your own opinion but as objective facts. Try to get the reader on your side by appearing reasonable or logical.

2 Paragraphs should be presented in a logical order. Each paragraph should present a point supporting the argument with evidence and examples that strengthen the case.

Begin each paragraph by relating it to the previous one and conclude with a lead in to the next point.

3 Reiteration – a summary of the arguments followed by a repetition of the opening assertion.

Generalise specific points to wider issues.

LANGUAGE FEATURES

- Use connectives associated with reasoning and causal links, e.g. therefore, consequently, furthermore, because of, moreover, in fact.

- Use simple, timeless, present tense for the argument but change tense if predictions are made (future) or if the past is discussed.

- Make use of the passive voice: it is believed, it can be said.

- Write about general participants: all dogs/teenagers/police officers rather than any particular one.

★ Brainstorm and link ideas before you start.

★ Spider diagrams are useful for linking your ideas.

★ Before you start construct a text plan using the steps above.

1 Persuasion – a written example

Is there too little time for play in the primary school day?

During the last decade there have been many changes to the school day brought about by the drive to raise standards in the British education system. Consequently, play opportunities have been restricted. Afternoon playtime has totally disappeared from many primary schools as teachers struggle with an ever fuller timetable. However, as crime and antisocial behaviour increases, the question is raised: 'Is it short-sighted to value purely educational development above the social and physical?' Indeed, can they be separated in this way?	The issue and main arguments. Generalising supports argument – 'many schools' rather than 'some schools'. Impersonal language strengthens case.
Barely a week goes by without media reports on the modern child's 'unhealthy lifestyle'. While the stereotype of children going home to slump in front of computer games or television programmes may be a generalisation, it must be true to say that nowadays fewer children are involved in physical, outdoor games than at any time in the last 100 years. In fact the British Heart Foundation warns that many children are laying the foundations for heart disease in adult life. Playtime is an ideal opportunity for children to exercise in a safe environment. In the school playground it is obvious that skipping, chasing, football and other physically challenging games are still enormously popular. Is it really acceptable that opportunities for such play be curtailed?	Point 1 – facts support persuasive comment. Counter arguments acknowledged but writer's side presented as far more reasonable to gain sympathy.
It could be argued that physical well-being is not the concern of schools. However, research shows that the best learning happens in short, concentrated bursts. Many children lose concentration during very long lessons and would benefit from a break to refresh them. In fact, learning sometimes continues in the playground as children discuss the lessons among themselves. Furthermore, playtime is an opportunity to develop imagination, and the ability to imagine is an important part of learning.	Point 2 – connected to previous paragraph. Argument developed and supported with evidence. Short sentences give emphasis. Longer sentences used for elaboration. Generalises about all children.
During playtime children develop other important life skills. They learn to share, argue, decide, lead, follow, be fair, invent rules and have fun with others. Some may say that playtime is an opportunity for bullying. However, the bullies will still be there before and after school even if all playtimes were stopped. Bullying must be dealt with but the answer is not preventing play opportunities where other children can learn vital social skills and develop their personalities.	Point 3 – develops the learning debate. Simple present tense used. Use of passive voice makes argument sound more objective and fair.
Although some people may fear that an increase in play opportunities in the school day would result in a lowering of educational achievement, this is not necessarily so. Healthy minds and bodies are better equipped for learning. Furthermore, playtime is an opportunity to improve the health and social behaviour of the next generation. It does seem as though there really is too little time for play in the primary school day.	Reiteration and summary of arguments.

2 Persuasion – a practice question

The following letter has been published in the local newspaper:

Dear Editor

I have just returned from a shopping trip to the town centre with my wife and feel compelled to write to you on the subject of young people and money. It seems to me that most young people nowadays have far too much pocket money and do nothing, or very little, to earn it. Their 'easy come, easy go' attitude is reflected by their 'spend, spend, spend' behaviour in the shops.

Surely it would be for the child's long term good if they had to earn their money, cleaning the house, doing the ironing and cutting the grass. If the job were not done properly, they shouldn't be paid. By working hard for their money they would learn to appreciate it more and would be less willing to squander every penny on shoddy fashion goods.

I fail to see why any child under the age of ten has the need for money at all. Surely their parents provide everything they need. Gifts at festivals and birthdays would be valued more if children were not getting new toys all the year round.

I intend to write an article on this subject for your newspaper, which I understand is read by many parents, in the near future. Hopefully we can begin to change this trend of swamping children with money and can return to a system where they learn the proper value of money.

Yours sincerely
George Wilson

The Question

You are very concerned by Mr Wilson's letter as you feel it does not fairly state the case for children being given a reasonable amount of pocket money. Write your own article for the newspaper entitled **'Children of today need pocket money'**. The purpose of your article is to persuade the readers that your position is a fair one.

- Brainstorm ideas. Plan your text into paragraphs using the steps on page 21.

- Refer back to the language features on page 21 before you start.

- When you have completed your article check it against the written example on page 22. Do you think it is a Level 5 answer?

WRITING FICTION

Fiction is imaginative narrative. The form could be any type of story, poem or play. The purpose of narrative is usually to entertain, but it can also explain, persuade or inform the reader. Narrative is written for all ages and the style and type of narrative will reflect its target readership.

In this section we will be looking at the distinctive features of different types of fiction.

- ⭐ Adventure and scary, suspense-style stories
- ⭐ Myths and legends
- ⭐ Fairy tales

Narrative features

The basic format of narrative text is:

Orientation

Creates a context for the story by giving information about:
- time
- place
- conditions
- one or more characters

A series of events leads to

Complication

- Developed using description of events and dialogue, which illuminate the characters and their different points of view.
- Often a good v. evil struggle in some way.

Complications build up as much as possible to a

Climax
Or crisis point

Story cannot move on without a

Resolution

- Sorting out or fixing of problem.
- Re-orientation of (at least) the major characters – how they have changed or been affected by the story.
- Often the triumph of good over evil.
- Must be believable to satisfy reader.

Adventure Stories

Definition

Adventure stories have a lot of action and suspense. They are written for entertainment and to take the reader into a different world/experience away from their normal day-to-day life.

To achieve Level 5 you should:

* not spend valuable time giving detail, description or dialogue that is unnecessary to the story line.

* use vocabulary precisely and effectively, to build up the tension and suspense in the story, and to create cliffhangers. Cliffhangers leave a situation or the main characters in terrible trouble, and do not immediately provide an answer. They are almost irresistible to the reader, and engage the reader's imagination most effectively.

TEXT PLAN

1 Orientation
Begin with brief information about time, place, conditions. Introduce the main character.

> **Where?** Walking home from school along a main road. Light dim.
> **Who?** Nathan and I.
> **Why?** Late home after chess club.

2 Opening events
Action or dialogue leading to action.

> See Laura from school.
> Arguing, pushing, pulling.
> Nathan calls out.

3 Series of events
Events or episodes – often small, unexpected complications – that lead the character(s) towards disaster.

> Laura bundled into red car.
> Josh appears. Agrees to chase. Jumps red light while in pursuit.

4 Complications continue
Plot unfolds rapidly and excitingly towards the climax.

> Followed by police then pulled over.
> Police agree to pursue.
> Hot car chase.

5 Resolution
Speedy conclusion which ties up loose ends of the story.

> Driver and accomplice run off but are caught.
> Nathan and I commended for bravery.

LANGUAGE FEATURES

- Write mostly in the past tense, occasionally moving forward into the present.
- Write in the 1st person (I, me) or 3rd person (he, she, it, they).
- Write chronologically, although you can use flashbacks.
- Use time connectives to reinforce the time sequence of the story, e.g. at first light, by lunchtime, then, later in the day, as night fell.
- Use connectives to redirect the reader's attention, e.g. just as that happened, meanwhile, and to produce suspense, e.g. without warning, abruptly.
- Use stereotypes for the setting/characters/events that will be known and understood by the reader, e.g. a stepmother (who is evil), a deserted, dark lane (which is dangerous).
- Use dialogue (all tenses).
- Use verbs to describe actions, but also feelings and thoughts.
- Use careful description to pull the reader in. Precise and effective use of adverbs, adjectives, metaphors and similes guide the reader on what to think or feel without necessarily telling them directly.

1 Adventure Stories – a written example

The Lucky Break

About two weeks ago, Nathan and I were walking home from chess club. It was pouring with rain, but we weren't in a hurry to get home and start our homework. We were chatting away about all sorts of things when Nathan suddenly stopped dead.	**Past tense.**
"Look," he stammered, "isn't that Laura from school?" We both peered into the gloomy evening. It certainly looked like Laura, the girl Nathan had fancied for a few weeks. She was with someone else, an adult, and they seemed to be arguing. We looked again. In the fading light it was quite hard to tell, but the hunched figure certainly did look like her. And judging by the rough movements made by the man, things were not going well.	
"Laura!" Nathan called, quite loudly I thought. But she didn't turn, didn't respond at all. "LAURA," he shouted more urgently this time. Still nothing from Laura. For a brief moment we watched, confused. Should we do something, try to intervene?	**Use of question to draw the reader in.**
Without warning, Nathan began to run towards her. The situation was obviously turning nasty, as the man had grabbed Laura and appeared to be shaking her. Nathan was calling out wildly, "Stop it, leave her alone, get off her." I didn't know what to do, so I ran blindly behind Nathan. My heart was beating like one thousand drums and beads of sweat had broken out on my brow. It was difficult to run – the pavements were greasy with the rain, and neither of us was dressed for a chase. I wondered, fleetingly, if we could actually do anything to help.	**Connective to create suspense.** **Suggestive but unclear language (builds suspense).** **Careful description including metaphor, adverbs and adjectives**

My thoughts were soon answered, for as we approached the corner a red car appeared. It was travelling very fast, but screeched to a halt very close to the couple. The side door flew open and the man bundled Laura inside. Within seconds the car was off again, the tyres screeching on the wet road.	**Connective to create suspense.**
Appalled, we turned to face each other. "What now?" I panted. "We can't let this go!" Nathan shook his head in despair. "How on earth can we catch the car when we couldn't even run fast enough to help in the first place?"	**Questions draw reader in. CLIFFHANGER**
Just then, a miracle happened. "Nathan, Nat," called a friendly voice. "D'you want a lift or what?" We turned and saw Nathan's brother Joe, the proud owner of a rusty old Mini. "Quick," yelled Nathan, as we piled into the Mini, "follow that red car down the road as fast as you can!" Fortunately, Joe loved a challenge.	**Connective to redirect attention. Questions that draw reader in.**
"You've got it," he drawled, and we sped off in hot pursuit.	
Minutes later we had the red car in sight. Joe was driving like a maniac – we were visibly shaking, but at least we were after them.	
As we closed the distance between the two cars, the traffic lights ahead of us began to change. "What shall I do?" shouted Joe. "Catch them, they've got Laura," we yelled. So we shot through the red lights, hot on the heels of our quarry.	
Meanwhile, the police car that had been sitting on a slip road by the lights started its engine and accelerated after us. It wasn't long before we realised – after all, a flashing blue light is quite an attention-seeker! Now we were being chased too.	**Connective to redirect attention.**
Within a few minutes, we had no choice. "I'm pulling over," Joe said firmly. "I'm not going to lose my licence over some school girl's row with her Dad." What could we say? After all, Laura hadn't shouted for help – were we actually sure she had been kidnapped, or could it be some kind of family problem?	**Questions that draw reader in.**
"Out you all get," a bulky policeman ordered, and we trooped out. "Now why would you need to be driving like that?" I suppose we were lucky he asked. I took a deep breath and quickly began to explain.	
"And so," I ended hurriedly, "Someone's got to stop the car. We could have lost them completely. Mind you, I suppose we have at least written down part of the number plate."	
"I see." There was a pause, as he weighed up our story. "OK, I'll call up the other squad cars. Maybe there's someone down the road who can pick them up."	

We listened in silence, and with heavy hearts, as he radioed ahead. Then we waited. It seemed like an eternity.

But suddenly the radio crackled.

CLIFFHANGER THEN CLIMAX
Connective to redirect attention

"There's been a lucky break...we've located the car...in pursuit now...oh, now we've got them..." And the voice stopped. We could hear all sorts of noise in the background and some yelling. What on earth had happened?

Speedy resolution, which ties up all the loose ends.

It wasn't until later that night – at home with our parents – that we heard the remainder of our adventure. The police had intercepted the red car and, in a top speed chase, it had somehow crashed into a tree. The two men had run off, but were caught after a few minutes. Laura was found, terrified, bound and gagged in the back of the car. And we were commended for our bravery in pursuing her captors. Fortunately, given the circumstances, Joe's red light incident was excused. But he did say he probably wouldn't bother to pick us up from school again. As for Nathan, well, let's just say the fact that he helped rescue Laura did wonders for his love life! As for me, well I'm never going to walk home alone.

Whole account is chronological.

KEY FACTS
- Suspense stories are very similar to adventure stories. If you are asked to write a suspense story, use the same planning format, with the pattern of orientation, complication and resolution.

- For suspense stories use more detailed and vivid descriptive detail. The setting would probably need to be creepy and it would probably be at night time! Develop characters and the plot so that the reader feels scared and anxious.

- The resolution in adventure and suspense stories should involve the clear triumph of good over evil, so the reader can feel relaxed in the end.

2 Adventure Stories – a practice question

The Question
Choose one of the following titles and write your own adventure story.
Make sure you re-read this chapter first so you use the right language features.

1. All of a sudden...
2. The end of the street
3. The daring raid
4. Around the corner
5. The deserted castle
6. The mysterious package
7. Another dawn
8. The hollow tree

★ Have you written a Level 5 answer? Check yours against the text plan and the language features on page 26.

★ If you need more practice, choose another title and start again.

Myths and Legends

Definition

Myths are anonymous. That means no one knows who wrote them. Their purpose is to explain natural events such as earthquakes, and religious beliefs such as why the world was created. They are tales of heroic adventures and often include supernatural beings!

To achieve Level 5, writers need to:

⭐ be able to use the simple structure effectively by choosing adverbs, metaphors and adjectives wherever possible.

⭐ use a 'story-telling' tone with vocabulary that is 'old fashioned' rather than informal and modern.

TEXT PLAN

1 Orientation
Should be brief and timeless, e.g. many ages ago.

Introduce generic characters.

Natural forces, such as fire, are represented as gods or god-like forms.

e.g. one animal represents all animals of that kind

2 Event and complications
Should happen quickly and involve conflict between characters.

Conflict usually involves two characters, e.g. between an animal and a god.

3 Resolution
Crucial to the 'story' as it needs to explain something significant about the world.

Resolution may involve supernatural powers but should make sense for the reader.

4 Conclusion
A summing up of the outcome.

e.g. And so to this day.

LANGUAGE FEATURES

- Write in the past tense, although dialogue may move into different tenses.
- Write in the 1st person (I, me) or 3rd person (he, she, they).
- Write chronologically, using time connectives, e.g. early that day, much later, as the sun was setting.
- Describe characters as either good or bad. Contrast between the two is an important part of the story.
- Use verbs to describe actions, but also thoughts and feelings of the characters.
- Use careful description to make an impact on the reader, with precise and effective use of adverbs, adjectives, metaphors and similes to guide the reader on what to think or feel without necessarily telling them directly.
- Use motifs, e.g. the youngest character is the hero or the most beautiful.
- Use some repetitive structure, e.g. but I'll huff and I'll puff…

1 Myths and Legends – a written example

How the hedgehog got its spikes

Long, long ago, at the beginning of the ages, animals were very different. All the animals were either smooth or furry, and everybody liked it that way. Animals in those days were friendly to everyone and spent their days not in hunting, but in playing wonderful games, or just enjoying the beauty of the world around them. The world was a peaceful, harmonious place and the gods looked down from their dwelling place above and were glad.

Timeless orientation. Story-telling tone.

However, one morning something happened that changed all that. Hedgehog awoke feeling irritable and decided that, instead of cheering himself up or spending some time on his own, he would take it out on the first animal he saw. As it happened, that animal was one of his dearest friends, Rabbit. "Hey, you," he called out, "the one with the ridiculous ears. Have you considered tying them back so they don't look so stupid?" Rabbit could not believe what he was hearing. Tears welled up in his eyes and he replied, "No, I've always rather liked them, for they are one of the things that make me special." And he ran off, as the tears started to fall down his little furry cheeks. Hedgehog laughed loudly and his laughter attracted the attention of Tree god. Tree god was not impressed by the unkind look in Hedgehog's eyes and decided to follow him secretly to find out what was going on.

Past tense with…

…dialogue in present.

Clear contrast between good and bad characters.

Unfortunately, he did not have long to wait. Hedgehog discovered that he liked the feeling he had after being unkind to Rabbit. So when he saw Duck waddling along, he called out loudly, "What's the matter with you? Can't you walk properly? Have your feet been crushed by a rock or something?" Just like Rabbit, Duck was stunned by the nasty tone. Once more, tears welled up. Duck was too horrified to reply and he too ran off as fast as he could, tears running down his little cheeks. Tree god was greatly saddened by Hedgehog's words and he started to muse about what should be done.

Careful description to draw in reader. Verbs explain feelings and actions.

As the days went on, Hedgehog became more and more unpopular. There was scarcely an animal that had not suffered his cruel taunts. Eventually, a

Time connective.

group of the animals went to visit the gods. "We are sorry to be a nuisance," they began, "but our lives are filled with sadness. Hedgehog's cruel words have cut into our hearts and we cannot live the way we did before. Is there nothing that could be done to stop him, or at least to warn animals he approaches that they need to get away quickly?" The gods agreed that Hedgehog was ruining their beautiful world by upsetting all the other animals, so they asked Tree god to solve the problem.

Story-telling tone.

One night, as Hedgehog was sleeping, Tree god sidled up carrying an armful of needles from the tallest pine tree in the forest. Slowly and carefully, he began sticking them into Hedgehog's beautiful smooth skin. Around each needle, the skin immediately swelled and turned red. All night Tree god worked and, when he had finished, he sat down near Hedgehog and waited for him to wake up.

Time connective.

Use of adverbs and adjectives heighten drama.

Next morning Hedgehog awoke in terrible pain. His body was throbbing where the needles had been placed. In anguish, he looked around for help and saw Tree god sitting close. "If you have any love in your heart for an animal in pain, please help pull these sharp needles out," he begged. "Indeed not," replied Tree god, "for it was me who stuck them there in the first place. And what is more, no matter how hard you try, you will never get them out. For each needle stands for an unkind or cruel comment you have made to another animal. It's time you learned your lesson, for now when you come into sight animals will be warned that your words can hurt. And you will constantly be reminded of the pain you have caused by the sharp needles you carry on your body."

Time connective.

Resolution clearly explained. The hedgehog has spikes because of his behaviour.

And so it was that all hedgehogs from that day have borne the needles, as a reminder to them and all who see them that unkind words always hurt someone and that sometimes the one who speaks the unkindness can be the one who suffers the most pain.

Moral of the story is a lesson that the reader needs to remember.

2 Myths and Legends – a practice question

The Question
Re-read the guidance on writing myths and then choose one of the following titles for your myth:

1. How the leopard got its spots.
2. Why the giraffe has a long neck.
3. Why the alligator has sharp teeth.
4. How the elephant got its trunk.
5. Why the reindeer has antlers.

⭐ Is your answer a Level 5 answer? Check against the structure and language features in this section.

⭐ If you need more practice try another title.

Fairy Tales

Definition

The main purpose of fairy tales is to entertain, but sometimes there is a moral to the story too, which aims to teach the reader an important truth. These stories are often culturally significant and their telling passes on traditional culture.

To achieve Level 5, writers need to:

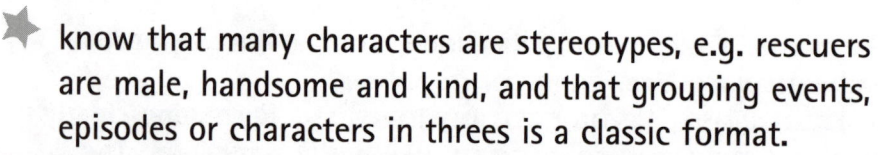

- know that there is an underlying moral message in fairy stories, i.e. know that honesty is always good and always rewarded!

- know that many characters are stereotypes, e.g. rescuers are male, handsome and kind, and that grouping events, episodes or characters in threes is a classic format.

- use description and detail to illuminate these characteristics. A Level 5 fairy story flows easily and feels familiar to the reader.

TEXT PLAN

1 Orientation
Describe the setting.
Introduce the main characters.

e.g. Once upon a time or Long, long ago etc.

2 Series of events
A series of events leading to at least one major complication.

Events should happen in quick succession. Start a new paragraph for each new event.

3 Complication
Should take up more than one paragraph.

There should be at least one major complication.

4 Resolution
All loose ends tied up.

Characters are allowed to live happily ever after!

LANGUAGE FEATURES

- Write in the past tense, although dialogue may move into different tenses.

- Write in the 1st person (I, me) or 3rd person (he, she, they).

- Write chronologically, using time connectives, e.g. early that day, much later, as the sun was setting.

- Describe characters as either good or bad. Contrast between the two is an important part of the story.

- Use verbs to describe actions, but also thoughts and feelings of the characters.

- Use careful description to make an impact on the reader, with precise and effective use of adverbs, adjectives, metaphors and similes to guide the reader on what to think or feel without necessarily telling them directly.

- Use motifs, e.g. the youngest character is the hero or the most beautiful.

- Use some repetitive structure, e.g. but I'll huff and I'll puff...

- Use groups of three: three bears, three pigs, three daughters, three wishes etc.

We haven't included any examples of fairy tales, as you will be more than aware of many of them. But, if you are asked to write a fairy story, as long as you remember to use the narrative planning format of Orientation, Complication and Resolution alongside the particular language features, you won't have any problems. Just keep in your mind the classic story language as you write and you will find you're using it too.

1 Fairy Tales – a practice question

The Question
Choose a couple of your favourite fairy stories. Read them and see if you can write the plan for them. Look out for the way the main complication is introduced and then resolved.

How many of the language features were you able to spot? Use the list above, and for each story re-read it and write down the features as you discover them. For example, look for and write down the connectives that show the passing of time. How many can you find in each story? Are the same connectives used in each story?

Reading Comprehension

Authors do not tell the reader everything. Through action, description and dialogue they show many aspects of the story. When reading a passage you have to work out what it is saying. You have to read between the lines.

> KEY FACT – To achieve Level 5 you must be able to
> READ BETWEEN THE LINES!!

Here are three examples to help you.

1 She stared wistfully into the shop window. | There is something she would like to buy or own but probably cannot BECAUSE that's what wistfully staring into a shop window usually implies.

2 Pulling on his hat, scarf and woollen gloves, he strode off into the night. | It's cold outside BECAUSE people wear hats, gloves and scarves in the cold.

3 Mina knelt down to welcome Fido, who came bounding up the path and covered her face with warm loving licks. | Mina already knows this dog and knows it's friendly BECAUSE people do not usually allow unfamiliar dogs to come close to their face or indeed cover them with licks.

Read between the lines and try to work out what is really being said.

1 "What a lovely hat!" she gushed with a patronising smile.

2 "It really doesn't matter," my auntie said, as she mopped anxiously at the tea dripping slowly on the beige carpet.

3 £2.50 was a fair price for the computer game but it was going to take him weeks to save that amount of money.

4 The yellowed pages felt fragile as he carefully turned them one by one.

Tip 1
It is important to answer the 1 mark questions very carefully but it is the 2 and 3 mark questions that will get you to Level 5!

Tip 2
Never explain a character's emotions or actions with a simple answer. Always support your point with examples from the text.

Tip 3
When answering a question about the author's intention be sure to talk about the vocabulary and style the author uses. (The sections on Sentences and Vocabulary later on in this book will help you.)

Tip 4
Only write about things in this question. Adding extra information will not earn you extra marks!

To achieve Level 5 you will need to be able to show that you can do all the following. Remember, you must always support your observations with at least one example from the text.

- Identify important details in the text.
- Recognise changes in mood through the text.
- Make deductions about characters, their emotions and motives.
- Identify the author's point of view from which a tale is being told or an argument made, and notice how that affects the telling.
- Compare different sections of the text and comment on each section.
- Recognise how the author uses techniques to influence the reader, e.g. keeping information hidden or presenting opinions as fact.
- Analyse how successfully the writer evokes feelings, such as sympathy or suspense, through vocabulary choices (such as similes) and sentence types.
- Identify different text types (pages 7 and 24 will remind you of these) and their purpose and language features.
- Compare and contrast texts.
- Use more than one source of information to support an answer. This could be extracting information from a chart or table and comparing it with a text.
- Express a personal preference supported with text examples. You must be able to explain and justify your ideas.

1 Reading Comprehension – practice questions

In your test you will be given a number of texts on the same theme. These may well include tables, charts, diagrams and poetry and plays. The marks you can earn for each question are shown on the test paper.

On the following pages there are two texts about chicken farming. Next to each piece of text are some typical examples of 2 and 3 mark questions for you to practise. We have added guidance notes to help you write an answer that will get you full marks.

Tip 5

When asked for your opinion or impression use the word BECAUSE and examples from the text that have led you to think this way.

Chat Show Chicken

The lights! The cameras! The fanfare! The curving steps! (I had a little trouble with the steps.) Then the wing-shake! And the green velvet sofa!

'Tonight, Viewers,' said my little green host proudly. 'Tonight – a great treat! A Chicken with a Mission. Not only does she not glow in the dark – Don't go away! We'll be seeing that later! – but she is here with a Message.'

He turned to me.

'Tell us the Message, Chicken.'

I turned to the cameras. I told them all the story of my life. I told them about the dreadful sheds, and who was in them now. I pointed out that it didn't even make sense.

'Why not?' my host demanded. 'After all, everyone has to eat.'

'Yes,' I said. 'But, you see, you're not just stuffed in the cages. While you're in the cages, you're stuffed! Stuffed with food.'

'What's wrong with that?' he demanded.

'What's wrong with that,' I told him and trillions of others, 'is that if you're going to be eaten (and it doesn't matter what you are – pig, chicken, calf, it's all the same) you have to grow. And to grow, you have to eat. In fact, you have to eat loads and loads to grow big enough for anyone to want to bother to eat you. So whoever ends up with you on their plate could just have eaten your food in the first place.'

'And what's your food?'

'Cereals and vegetables.'

He made a face.

'Boring old cereal and vegetables!'

I ignored him.

'And then they could have invited a whole crowd of other hungry people to join them. Because if you're going to be eaten you have to eat practically ten whole fields full of corn and stuff to make as much good food out of yourself as there was in just one of those fields to begin with.'

'Really?' my little green host said, stifling a yawn. 'I wonder how many viewers knew that.'

He turned to the camera.

'Hello, out there!' he said. 'Calling all hungry viewers! It looks as if the chicken's Message is as follows. Gang up with nine others. Pounce on one meat-eater. Force the meat-eater to eat fields instead. And all your problems will be over.'

And he fell off his green sofa, laughing.

I never thought my Mission would be easy. Indifference. Danger. Ridicule. Chickens of History must face them all. I could have sulked. I could have pushed the microphone aside with my wing and strutted off the set in disgust. I could have wept. But no.

I kept my head and my dignity.

'I see I'm not getting my Message over too well,' I told my little green host. 'So allow me to offer your viewers something more on their wavelength. I'll show them how I don't glow in the dark.'

The green glint in his eyes said:

'Now that's a bit more like it, Chicken. That might just save this wash-out show.'

His soft honey voice said:

'That would be wonderful, wouldn't it, Viewers?'

I fluttered down from the sofa and spread my wings.

The studio lights dimmed.

'Now I need total darkness, please.'

Suddenly there was total darkness.

In it, I silently, sadly, crept away.

Taken from *The Chicken Gave It To Me* © Anne Fine 1992.

READING COMPREHENSION

1. Find three phrases that show how the interviewer's feelings change during the interview.

   These questions test that you are able to find important details in the text and notice character changes as the story develops.

2. Some words and phrases indicate that the interviewer is not taking the chicken's views seriously. Find two and explain your choice.

   The word 'indicate' says that you are going to have to interpret these phrases.

3a. The chicken thought she might have to face indifference and ridicule on her mission. Did this happen during her interview? Use the text to explain your answer.

   For a Level 5 answer you must include examples from the text and an explanation of how these ridicule or show indifference.

3b. Explain how you think the chicken feels at this point in the story.

   To answer this you must go beyond what is actually written. You have to predict her feelings from the character that has been built up. You MUST back up arguments with evidence from the text.

4. Why is a capital M used for Mission and Message? What impact does it have on the reader?

   This answer will show that you recognise how presentation and organisation contribute to the effect.

5. Find the part in the story beginning 'The green glint in his eyes....' What does this section tell us about the interviewer's mood and behaviour at this time?

   The question refers to mood and behaviour implying there is a difference, so your answer must refer to both and find reasons for the difference.

6. The chicken does not think the interview went well. Was the interviewer fair?   yes   no
   What makes you think this? Explain your reasons using parts of the story to help you.

   This question asks you to go beyond the text and use what you know about TV interviews. You may use phrases like 'a fair interviewer would... but this one....'

7. This chapter is a diary entry written by the chicken. In two or three sentences, write a diary entry for the interviewer describing the programme.

   This question is testing whether you understand how the point of view from which a tale is told affects the telling.
   AND
   To plot changes as they develop through a narrative.

2 Reading Comprehension – Text 2

17, Station Drive,
Lower Thicket,
Herts.

12th September 2000

Dear Editor,

While searching the Internet earlier today the headline 'Farmers told to treat chickens better' immediately caught my eye. The article that followed was not disappointing. It reported that the major fast food restaurants in the USA have issued strict guidelines to their suppliers on the way egg farmers are to care for their hens in future. This news was so very heartening that I felt compelled to share it with your readers.

The hens are to be given cages that are 50% larger, which means that they will have enough space to lie down and will have easier access to food and water. A second change is that the practice of de-beaking, which is done to prevent the birds pecking each other, will be phased out. Company inspectors will visit the farms to see that these changes are carried out.

Some of your more extreme readers may think these changes do not go far enough, and indeed it is true that the animals will need even more space to be able to spread their wings. However, I believe they reflect a trend that is leading steadily towards more humane animal farming. The major restaurant chain involved buys 1.5 billion eggs yearly. These policy changes will certainly improve the lives of the millions of hens; and it will do it right now! More extreme changes would be very costly and a major restructuring of the farms would be necessary. There is little chance of that happening in the very near future so let us welcome each small improvement.

The USA has lagged behind Europe where the living conditions of farm animals are concerned. All chicken caging is to be phased out in countries that are part of the European Union by the year 2012. Cruelty in farming is becoming a world-wide issue. Although the US has not yet passed any laws such as the European one, interest in the treatment of farm animals is increasing. At present about 3% of eggs sold in the USA are free range, from hens that are not kept in cages, and this percentage is increasing. Everything points to this move by the fast food restaurant chains being an important step along the path to humane living conditions for chickens.

Surely we must congratulate these companies and celebrate this advance for our cause. This move, which must be costing the companies serious money, deserves our support.

Yours sincerely,

Anita Thompson

SUPERMARKET SURVEY OF NON-BATTERY EGGS SOLD IN BRITISH SUPERMARKETS

Nine major supermarket chains responded to the survey carried out by the leading farm animal welfare group, Compassion in World Farming.

NB These figures represent the proportion of non-cage alternatives to battery eggs sold by the major supermarket companies that responded to CIWF's survey during January–April 1998. They are a percentage of the total number of eggs sold.

Supermarket	Percentage
ASDA	36%
Budgens	18%
CWS (Co-op)	37%
Marks & Spencer	100%
Safeway	52%
Sainsbury's	31%
Somerfield	25%
Tesco	20%
Waitrose	65%

1a What was Anita Thompson's reaction to the article **'Farmers told to treat chickens better'**?

1b Find three words or phrases in the letter that make you think this.

Answer each part separately. 1a should be answered using different words from those in the text.

2 Is the aim of Anita's letter to share the information she read on the Internet or is she trying to persuade the readers of a particular point of view?

You need to identify the writer's technique. Which non-fiction text type is she using?

3 Anita thinks that the **'more extreme readers'** who **'may think these changes do not go far enough'** are wrong. Explain as fully as you can why she thinks this.

You must not simply quote passages from the letter. Try to show why she welcomes the changes and why she thinks not to do so is wrong.

4 '3% of eggs sold in the USA are free range.' What does Anita Thompson think this indicates and how does she use this information to support her argument?

There are two questions here – be sure to answer both. Try to bring the European point into the answer.

5 Anita Thompson claims that 'The USA has lagged behind Europe where the living conditions of farm animals are concerned.' Is this a fair comment? Use the table provided to help you decide.

This question is a chance to show how you can use information from more than one source to support an answer.

6 Anita Thompson used the information from the table to add a PS to her letter but this was not published. It began 'Recently released statistics...'.
Complete the PS in a way that she might have written it.

You will need to summarise the table and compare it to the US. (Note the dates!) Use the information to strengthen Anita's argument.

Sentences

Definition

Sentences are made up of one or more clauses. A clause is a group of words containing a subject and a verb. A clause will convey:

* an event
* a situation

Sentences fall into three main types

Simple	one clause	He hit the brakes.
Compound	two or more clauses linked by a conjunction	He hit the brakes but the car slid into the frozen ditch. The clauses are equally important and could stand alone as two separate sentences.
Complex	main clause has information added to it by subordinate clause	While his hands gripped the wheel, he hit the brakes. The subordinate clause cannot make a sentence on its own but relies on the main clause (he hit the brakes) for its meaning.

KEY FACT
Level 5 writers use a variety of sentence types. Look at this example:

> *He was an old hand at air raids now.*
> *As the yell of the sirens climbed the sky he came smoothly out of his dreams. Not scared. Only his stomach clamped down tight for action, as his hands found his clothes laid ready in the dark.*

Kingdom by the Sea, by Robert Westall, Mammoth, 1992

In this extract Robert Westall creates suspense and anticipation by using different sentence types.

SIMPLE SENTENCES

Simple sentences can be powerful.

- They can create suspense, mystery or excitement.
- They can leave the reader wanting more.
- They can create surprise by signalling a change in events.
- They can add emphasis to an argument.

1 Simple Sentences – practice questions

1. The following sentences are taken from adventure stories. Write a simple sentence to complete each of these paragraphs, leaving the reader wanting to know more.

    a) It was as if the whole room was rapidly closing in on him, as if the air was being squeezed from his aching lungs.

    b) The book must be hidden in a safe place; somewhere nobody else would even imagine.

    c) The car slowed to a halt and a woman's head peered from the darkened window as it smoothly unwound.

2. Change the mood of these sentences by adding a simple sentence.

    a) With so many secret nooks and crannies the garden should have been magical but Paul was far too glum to notice.

    b) Sunlight danced on the water, turning winter gloom into warmth and happiness.

    c) He felt himself going redder and redder as Mum entertained 'the aunties' with stories of his baby days.

3. Emphasise these points with a concluding short sentence.

    a) Despite the very well publicised dangers, many drivers ignore the risks and continue to drive while using mobile phones.

    b) However, it is still possible to see dogs roaming, off the lead, in children's play areas, causing distress and danger to many youngsters.

    c) Indeed dentists recommend that children under the age of seven should be supervised when cleaning their teeth.

4. Rewrite these simple sentences to emphasise the WAY the things were done. Start with the adverb.

    a) The door creaked open slowly.

    b) The children formed a line noisily.

    c) Sam tiptoed stealthily across the living room.

COMPOUND SENTENCES

Compound sentences bring ideas together.

- They link two or more simple sentences to create a longer one.

- Compound sentences can sound better than two simple sentences, e.g.

    The bird flew back to her treetop nest. She began to feed the hungry chicks.

    may sound better as

    The bird flew back to her treetop nest and began to feed the hungry chicks.

2 Compound Sentences – practice question

1. Create a compound sentence from these simple sentences using the best conjunction you can.

    a) My Grandpa's house has two spare bedrooms. I've got to share my sister's room.

    b) The day began well. It got worse and worse.

    c) The ducks were very well fed. They waddled contentedly about the park.

    d) Tom knew he had a late night before him. He had been up until midnight the previous day.

COMPLEX SENTENCES

To achieve Level 5, writers MUST be able to control complex sentences to create interest and variety in their writing.

- Complex sentences link ideas together and show the relationship between them.
  Despite the rain, everybody turned up on time.

- The first word of the subordinate clause often shows how the ideas are related.
  Examples are: despite, although, when, before, after, since, until, because
  He wore light summer clothes, although the weather was bitterly cold.

- Subordinate clauses can start a sentence to create variety and different effects.
  Since taking part in the London Marathon, Petros had become a running enthusiast.

- Slipping a subordinate clause in after a noun can add detail or description.
  The house, which stood at the end of a magnificent drive, had an abandoned feel.

3 Complex Sentences – practice questions

1. Add a subordinate clause to the end of these main clauses to create complex sentences.

   a) Mr Wilson slept soundly until ten o'clock.

   b) Sam and Jem had always been good friends.

   c) It is often said that cats have nine lives.

2. Add a subordinate clause to the start of these sentences to make them more interesting.

   a) The amount of litter in town centres is increasing.

   b) Britain remains one of the few countries to drive on the left.

   c) He missed his home and family terribly.

3. Add a subordinate clause after the noun. Look at the example to see how to use commas in this sentence type.

   a) The parcel stood temptingly on the table.

   b) The puppy gnawed mischievously on Dad's slipper.

   c) Snuggled up in her bed she wondered if she would do the same again.

> **Tip**
> Any sentence type is monotonous if overused. To achieve Level 5 you will need to vary word order and sentence type to maintain the reader's interest.

Varying sentence type is a great technique to use when writing narrative. Look at these two examples and see how the authors have used different sentence types:

David Almond – 'Skellig'

He was lying there in the darkness behind the tea chests, in the dust and the dirt. He was filthy and pale and dried out and I thought he was dead. I couldn't have been more wrong. I'd soon begin to see the truth about him, that there had never been another creature like him in the whole world.

Skellig (2nd Edition), by David Almond, Hodder Children's Books, 1998

The author has used all three sentence types when introducing us to Skellig for the first time.

Gillian Cross – 'The Demon Headmaster'

As they sat over their tea, Dinah was even quieter than usual. She gazed into her cup, watching the brown liquid swirl around, and Mrs Hunter had to ask her three times whether she wanted another piece of cake.
'Sorry.' She looked up at last.

The Demon Headmaster, by Gillian Cross, Puffin, 1984

In 'The Demon Headmaster' Gillian Cross often starts complex sentences with the subordinate clause.

Practice questions

1. Think of a character you are going to write about. Writing in the first person (using I), compose a paragraph to introduce your character.

    a) Write where the character was and what they were doing when you first saw them.

    b) Use a compound sentence for a brief physical description AND your reaction.

    c) Hint at things to come in the story with a simple sentence.

2. Imagine a character with something on their mind. Decide on a setting (but not the tea table). Write a short paragraph containing a variety of sentence types in which your character's mood is shown by their actions and the reactions of those around them.

⭐ Re-read what you have written. Are you happy with the way it introduces the character?

⭐ Would changing the word order of any of the sentences improve what you have written?

Paragraphs

Paragraphs organise the writing so that it is easy to read and understand.

> The simple rule is: A NEW IDEA = A NEW PARAGRAPH

Starting a new paragraph shows the reader that the narrative is moving to a different phase. It shows something has changed. That could be:

- Time has moved on or back.
- A new location.
- A new character is introduced.
- Something new is happening.
- A flashback.
- A new speaker in a passage of dialogue.

Paragraphs – an example

The weather outside was miserable and the skies were thick with rain clouds.

Amina thundered into the kitchen. 'Isn't dinner ready yet? I'm starving,' she moaned. Her mother looked up wearily, and sighed as she shook her head. — **New paragraph:** Something new is happening

'Amina!' scolded her father 'Can't you see your mother is not feeling well? Please show some consideration.' — **New paragraph:** Her father speaks

'What's wrong?' Amina asked anxiously. — **New paragraph:** Amina speaks

KEY FACT

Paragraphs are very important in non-fiction writing too. Use the step by step plans in Section 1 to guide you.

Tip 1
A new idea = a new paragraph.

Tip 2
Plan your paragraphs before you start. This will help you remember to begin new paragraphs when you do start writing.

The Passive Voice

Definition
The passive voice is a way of hiding the someone or something (called the agent) that causes the action. To achieve Level 5, writers need to know how and when to use the passive voice and, when appropriate, include it in the variety of sentences they use.

When to use the passive voice

When it does not matter who did the action.	The milk was delivered early.	Good writers leave out unnecessary details.
If you don't want to tell who the agent is or was.	The Ming vase was smashed.	Good writers keep information back from the reader.
When you want to focus on who it was done to and not who did it.	Mother had been stabbed.	Focusing on the recipient of the action can create powerful effect.
To create a powerful argument and make it sound fairer.	it is estimated it is believed are caused by	By not disclosing **who** estimates, it sounds as if everyone would come up with this estimation – it generalises.
When writing impersonal reports, such as science experiments.	The plant was placed in a dark cupboard for two weeks.	It doesn't matter who did this; the results should be the same for everyone.

Writing active sentences

⭐ Sentences containing active verbs are usually presented like this:

Someone or something	does something to	someone or something
Heavy traffic	ruins	the countryside.
The man	followed	the children.

Writing passive sentences

⭐ When written in the passive voice the sentence is turned around.

⭐ 'By' is often used to introduce the agent after the passive verb.

| The countryside | is ruined | by heavy traffic. |
| The children | were followed | by the man. |

Tip
Use the passive voice carefully! In narrative writing it is a tool to create hooks for the reader. BUT DON'T OVERDO IT! The active voice is by far the most common.

The Passive Voice – a practice question

Re-write the following sentences in the passive voice.

1 The angry dog attacked the teenage crowd.

2 The wolf had eaten Grandma.

3 The bull elephant leads the charge.

4 Paul saved the drowning child.

5 Sarah kicked the football through the stained glass window.

Now re-read your passive sentences. Do some of them sound clumsy? Sometimes the passive voice should be avoided!

KEY FACTS
When using the passive voice you can create powerful sentences by 'hiding the agent'. For example:

The man followed the children!	Active voice – a good sentence
The children were followed by the man!	Passive voice – a clumsy sentence
The children were followed!	Passive voice without the agent – a good sentence!

- Re-read your passive voice sentences from the practice question.

  Which ones sound better without the agent?

- Re-write these in the passive voice with the agent hidden!

Tip
Level 5 writers use a variety of sentence types!

Vocabulary

When choosing vocabulary remember every word counts!

⭐ Vocabulary choices need to be **precise**, **accurate** and **imaginative**.

⭐ Choosing words is like telling a joke: even the best shouldn't be used too often or they will lose their impact.

ADJECTIVES

Definition
Adjectives come before or after a noun; they describe somebody or something. They can create powerful description but take care not to overuse them and to use them accurately.

The verb *fought* creates a powerful picture, gripping the reader's attention.	The cliffs *fought* with the waves from the **rippling** sea, roaring to be successful.	Look at the adjective! More accurate alternatives might be: • **rough** • **choppy** • **storm-tossed**

⭐ You should never use two adjectives with the same meaning in one phrase, e.g.

  The rough, bumpy path

⭐ Two adjectives may be used if they both add useful detail to the story, e.g.

  The steep, rough path   OR   *The lonely, rough path*   (Two very different paths!)

⭐ **Danger!!** Never use common adjectives, e.g. *okay, great, really, boring,* from speech in your writing unless they are quotes or in dialogue.

  Dolphins are really interesting is not a good sentence.
  Dolphins are fascinating is a Level 5 description!

⭐ An accurate noun is often better than a string of adjectives or an adjectival phrase.

  The doctor, who was going to perform the operation, strode into the room.
  would be better as...
  The surgeon strode into the room.

⭐ Adjectives work well when they alliterate (start with the same sound).

Adjectives – practice questions

1. **Change some of the adjectives in these sentences for more accurate ones.**

   a) The bull elephant charged at the party of tourists, glaring angrily with bright eyes.

   b) The storm raged and fluffy clouds charged about in the wild sky.

   c) The ball slammed into the net and the pleased supporters gave a yell of triumph.

   d) The raft was swept along the meandering river.

2. **Use two different adjectives to support each of these nouns (e.g. the quaint, pink cottage). Think of the picture you are trying to create.**

   a cottage   a horse   a market square   a teacher   feet   dogs

   Try each noun twice and create different pictures each time.

3. **Turn these into appropriate written sentences by changing the adjective.**

   a) The news was pretty boring.

   b) I watched a great movie last night.

   c) The uniform was okay but the hat didn't fit.

   d) The shop was full of really great clothes.

4. **Try to find specific nouns for the following:**

   a) A graceful sailing boat

   b) Someone carrying bags and suitcases

   c) An expensive sports car

   d) The metal disc with his name and address on

5. **Find the second adjective to an make alliterative phrase with each of these:**

   a) the golden crown

   b) a pink rose

   c) the tousled child

   d) the shiny knife

ADVERBS

Definition

Adverbs can be used to tell how something was done.

*The old man climbed **slowly** and **painfully** up the winding stairs.*

Adverbs – a practice question

Improve these sentences with adverbs.

a) Anna poured the hot tea.

b) The car was reversed into the drive.

c) The ducks swam on the polluted pond.

d) On the count of four she leaped onto the box.

VERBS

Clear and interesting writing is often achieved through the use of powerful verbs.

Jack jumped up and rapidly pulled tins and packets out of the cupboard.
OR
Jack jumped up and rummaged through the cupboards.

The second sentence would be the choice of a Level 5 writer!

⭐ Don't tell the reader what to feel; make them feel it themselves through the 'description'.

⭐ Look how many powerful verbs David Almond used to create this powerful description.

The door creaked and cracked a moment before it was still. Dust poured through the torch beam. Something scratched and scuttled in the corner. I tiptoed further in and felt spider webs breaking on my brow.

Skellig (2nd Edition), by David Almond, Hodder Children's Books, 1998

Tip

It's not necessary to use phrases like 'It was scary' if your descriptions are powerful enough. Your description makes suggestions for the reader's mind to work on.

Here are some more useful vocabulary choices:

REPETITION

This is a useful tool for building atmosphere or suspense. Repetition often works well in short phrases, e.g.

> *Fog everywhere. Fog up the river, fog down the river. Fog on the Essex marshes, fog on the Kentish heights. Fog in the eyes and throats of the Greenwich pensioners wheezing by the firesides.*
>
> From '**Bleak House**' by Charles Dickens

SIMILE

This creates an image in the reader's mind by comparing a subject to something else. The comparison is often made by using the words AS or LIKE and frequently exaggerates.

> *It was as if the fires of the sun burned in his face.*
>
> *Her eyes sparkled like sunlight on water.*

METAPHOR

This describes a subject by writing as if it really is something else. A metaphor can sound stronger than a simile.

> *The twins were a hurricane leaving a trail of destruction behind them.*
>
> *A river of tears streamed down the old woman's face.*

KEY FACTS

Examiners are looking to see if you can make good vocabulary choices, so show them that you can! Have a go at the word. If you use all of your spelling knowledge there is a good chance you will get it right. And if not, you will gain more marks for good vocabulary than you will lose for a wrong spelling.

Spelling

Your spelling will be assessed in the Spelling Test. This is the only time that your spelling will be specifically marked. The Spelling Test aims to check your spelling skills by asking you to spell particular words within a piece of text.

The test will cover:

- basic spelling rules that you probably already know.
- more difficult or unusual words that might not conform to a rule.

Work through the spelling rules that follow and make sure you understand them. They will help you to do well if you learn them properly.

KEY FACTS

This is a list of the 20 most frequently misspelt words in the SATs test last year. Make sure you get them right this year!

change	technique
advertise	swimming
injured	ready
serious	vanishing
surprise	known
nastiest	stripes
designed	perfectly
regardless	future
attempts	produce
individual	themselves

PLURALISATION (making plurals)

There are several different rules when you are making plurals.

1 Most words just need you to add 's'. For example: dog – dogs, hat – hats, table – tables.

2 Words that end with a hissing or buzzing sound need you to add 'es', or they sound and look funny. For example: fox – foxes, church – churches, wish – wishes, guess – guesses, buzz – buzzes. So, words ending in x, z, ch, sh or s normally follow this rule.

3 Words that end in 'y' have their own rules. If the letter before the 'y' is a VOWEL (a, e, i, o, u), you just add 's'. For example: boy – boys, toy – toys, key – keys. But, if the word ends in 'y' and has a CONSONANT (all the other letters that aren't vowels) before the 'y' you need to **drop the 'y'** and **add 'ies'**. For example: baby – babies, story – stories, fly – flies.

4 Words that end in 'lf' sometimes need you to change the 'f' to 'ves'. For example: wolf – wolves, self – selves, but not gulf – gulfs.

5 You need to be aware of the irregular plurals too, e.g. child – children, woman and man – women and men, mouse – mice.

Pluralisation – practice questions

1 Make these singular words into plurals:

House, jug, phone, lunch, push, box, computer, mat, penny, knife, wall, zoo, pony, packet.

Design a table to show which words belong to which spelling group.

2 **Collect as many different words as you can that end with Y, X, Z, S.**

Write them down in their singular form and then as plurals.

DOUBLING THE CONSONANT

When you are adding 'ing', 'er', 'ed' or 'en', there is a rule to help you decide if you need to double the consonant or not. The trick is to know what type of sound the vowel is making!

Vowels can make two sounds:
- they can say their name and make a long sound, e.g. 'a' in play.
- they can say a short sound, e.g. 'a' in cat.

The basic rule is: double the letter if the vowel makes a short sound, e.g. mat – matting, pat – patting, thin – thinned, pet – petted.

Doubling the consonant – a practice question

Do these words have long or short vowel sounds?
Table, pin, pine, hit, nail, pig, cat, dog, fox, frame, pen, boot, mend, hole, cot, cave, mute, mutter.

- Make a chart showing which are long sounds and which are short. Can you add any more?
- Now take the word list above and add 'er', 'ed', 'er' or 'ing' depending on the word. Some of the words can be written with several of those endings.
- Have you spelt them correctly by checking the length of the vowel sound before deciding whether or not to double the consonant?
- Check your spellings in a dictionary.

LONG VOWELS

Long vowels are important because in each case there are several different ways of spelling the same sound.

A: 'ai' as in pain; 'ay' as in lay; 'a-e' as in snake. 'ai' usually comes in the middle of words, and 'ay' and 'a-e' usually come at the end. If you listen carefully, you can hear the extra sound of the 'y'. If you can hear it, it will help you make the right spelling choice.

E: 'ee' as in kneel; 'ea' as in reach; 'ie' as in grief; 'e-e' as in here.

I: 'i-e' as in time; 'y' as in fly; 'igh' as in might. Most use 'i-e'.

O: 'o-e' as in tone; 'oa' as in float; 'ow' as in blow. 'oa' usually comes in the middle of words, and 'ow' and 'o-e' usually come at the end.

U: 'u-e' as in tube; 'oo' as in loot; 'ew' as in knew. 'u-e' and 'ew' usually come at the end of a word, and 'oo' usually comes in the middle.

Now take each vowel and for each vowel sound, list as many words as you can which have that spelling pattern. You will find some exceptions as you work, so make sure that you make a note of them so they don't catch you out.

APOSTROPHES OF POSSESSION AND OMISSION

These apostrophes are the cause of many punctuation and spelling mistakes! All you need to do to get the word right is to pause a little before adding the apostrophe.

Possession

- **The possessive apostrophe is used to show something belongs to someone or something.** For example: Tamsin's make-up – the make-up belonging to Tamsin; Helen's car – the car belonging to Helen.

- **Notice what happens to the possessive apostrophe when the noun is a plural.** For example: the boys' coats – the coats belonging to the boys (plural); the boy's coat – the coat belonging to the boy (singular).

- **Ask yourself before adding the apostrophe: 'Is there an object here that actually belongs to someone?'** If so, then use the apostrophe.

Omission

- **The apostrophe of omission is used when a letter has been omitted or left out.** For example: has not – hasn't; would not – wouldn't; she has – she's; it is – it's.

- **If it helps, say the two words aloud to check if you have used the apostrophe correctly.**

Apostrophes – a practice question

1 Now practise using the apostrophe of omission by changing these words.

   Would not, could not, should not, cannot, will not, he has, they have, we have.

2 Look for some more examples of apostrophe use in your books. Can you list them as either possessive or of omission?

Tip 1
When you're preparing for your tests, write down any words you find especially tricky. Try to learn them using the Look, Cover, Write, Check approach. Also try writing them in sentences so you can keep them in context, as this can help too.

Tip 2
Always segment a word you are trying to spell if you don't immediately know it. Split the word into syllable blocks and try to work out each section. Apply any spelling patterns that you know in each section, e.g. always use 'u' after 'q', even if you aren't sure you can do the whole word this way.

If you still feel unsure, HAVE A GO ANYWAY! You won't lose much if you get it wrong, and you might even get it right.

Punctuation

Punctuation is the tool by which you tell the reader HOW to read your work: when to pause, what to stress, what is questioned and what is exclaimed. Writers hear their words inside the heads with all of these features but it is only through punctuation that anyone else will know how the words should be said.

⭐ **Punctuation is vital to a clear and dynamic writing style.**

⭐ **'No!' is quite different from 'No?', which in turn is different from 'No...'.**

SENTENCES – the basics

To achieve Level 5, writers need to remember that:
- every sentence begins with a capital letter and ends with a full stop. If it's a question, it must have a question mark
- names of people and places must have a capital letter, as do days of the week, months and organisation names.

You should already know these facts really well. But take care – it would be silly to lose marks on the easy bits, like sentences.

COMMAS

Commas are used to separate ideas in sentences. When you say a sentence you are going to write, you can usually feel where the commas go by the pause or change of tone in your voice.

Leah, who was very late, crept into class.

The cat was in a basket, but it still scratched the dog.

Commas also separate items in a list or a series of describing words. For example:

- **Lists of names** – The goals were scored by Sam, Robyn, Karim and Mehmet.

- **Lists of adjectives** – The children were cold, wet and very frightened.

- **Lists of instructions** – You will need the following: some scrap paper, scissors, masking tape, string and an egg box.

Commas – practice questions

Put the commas in these sentences.

a) Although the tickets were greatly reduced few children could afford them.

b) Before the lesson can begin the young riders are kitted out with a well-fitting helmet.

c) The fox who used to be regarded as a nocturnal animal is being spotted more and more in city gardens during daytime.

d) The shoes fitted well but by the evening her feet were killing her.

SPEECH MARKS

Speech marks are the writer's way of showing when a character is speaking.

- They separate the author's voice from the characters' voices.

- Authors frequently break up speech by putting details of who is speaking in among words. In longer sections of speech this is a good technique to use. Speech written in this way needs two sets of speech marks.

Speech Marks – some examples

"If you don't leave me alone, I'll scream," Tony yelled.

Speech marks go at the start of the speech.
Speech marks go at the end of speech.
If you don't leave me alone, I'll scream
This is in speech marks because they are the words Tony yelled.

Laura whispered, "The blue one was grandma's."

Notice where the comma goes when the sentence starts with Laura whispered.
The spoken words always start with a capital letter.

"Do you really expect me to believe that story?" Mother asked.

Full stops, commas, question marks and exclamation marks go inside the speech marks.

"Stop!" he screamed.

"Get up Lucy," mother sighed, "it's nearly seven thirty."

The words mother spoke are all one sentence so the second section of speech does not begin with a capital letter.

"It's six more days until my birthday," Terry said. "What are you getting me?"

If more than one sentence is spoken it looks like this.

OTHER LEVEL 5 PUNCTUATION

To achieve Level 5, you must show the use of other punctuation that 'adds voice' to your writing. Try using the following:

- **Colon** – Two dots, one above the other. Used to introduce a list.

    The following are all mammals: cow, dog, human.

- **Ellipsis** – Three dots ... Used to show there is a long pause or something is missed out.

    "It's gone..." her voice trailed off, as she realised the implications of the loss.

- **Dash** – Shown as a line – . Used to add an afterthought.

    My great aunt was evil and – there's really no polite way to put this – smelly!

A practice question

Put the punctuation in this passage. Everything has been left out, not just speech marks. You must read to the end of the passage before starting this activity. Notice how hard it is to read unpunctuated writing. That's another reason why examiners love punctuation!

twenty five pence is a lot to pay for an old bus ticket tom remarked trying to stifle the laughter that was bubbling up inside him not for a beauty like this it isnt old mac replied lovingly smoothing out the ticket are you a collector or something then I could be described as that muttered old mac but its not the name I give myself well what are you then tom enquired getting interested a public transport historian the old man declared proudly thats what I am a public transport historian

Handwriting

From 2003 your handwriting will be assessed through your two Writing tests. Below are examples of work awarded 3, 4 or 5 marks (out of 5). Have a good look at them and try to write in your best handwriting every time you do an activity from this book. How would you do? Try with different pencils and pens so that you are sure which tool gives you the best result. Remember, any crossings out may lose you marks, so rub out if you need to using a clean rubber.

Writing awarded 3 marks has letters that are always accurately formed and are consistent in size. It is partly joined or printed, and the letters and words are suitably spaced.

The writing below has been given 3 marks.

> *Henry shuffled slowly over to his mother, "Mum, I have to go and join the Light Brigade," he whispered.*

Writing awarded 4 marks is legible and joined, with the correct joins between letters. The ascenders (tall parts of the letter above the line) and descenders (tall parts of the letter below the line) are in proportion and parallel. Spacing between the words and letters is consistent.

The writing below has been given 4 marks.

> *Henry shuffled slowly over to his mother, "Mum I have to go and join the light Brigade," he whispered.*

Writing awarded 5 marks is controlled, confident and stylish, with consistency in joins, size and spacing all the way through. There are no crossings out and no obvious pauses in the writing. There are also no copying errors – if you get 5 marks, you will have taken care to get it exactly right.

The writing below has been given 5 marks.

> *Henry shuffled slowly over to his mother, "Mum, I have to go and join the Light Brigade," he whispered.*

Test Technique

Don't forget to have breakfast in the morning – if you haven't got time, eat a banana on the way to school.

Always skim read the whole paper before you start, so that there are no surprises.

Writing

1. Read through all the options before choosing your task. Don't just do the first one because you can. You want to choose the one that you can complete the best, so choose carefully.

2. Use all of your planning time. You will have 15 minutes and a basic planning format that will nudge you in the right direction. Use the detailed text plans in this book to help you. Planning is crucial if you are going to produce a well-shaped and properly organised piece of writing. Note down key vocabulary, language features, suitable connectives etc. when you have filled in the main structure of your plan. When you think you have finished, start composing paragraph units. PLANNING TIME IS NEVER WASTED TIME.

3. Enjoy the writing time, and enjoy showing off what you know. Level 5 writers are confident and, if you have enjoyed writing, your work will reflect this and be of a higher standard.

4. Try to leave yourself five minutes at the end of your writing to check what you have written and to ensure it really says what you want it to say. Improve your vocabulary choices if necessary, and check for correct paragraphing and punctuation.

5. Read well before the tests – all types of books, including picture ones for older children. The language choices they make will help shape yours. Good writers spend a lot of time reading because it gives them ideas and vocabulary, and it's a brilliant way to relax!

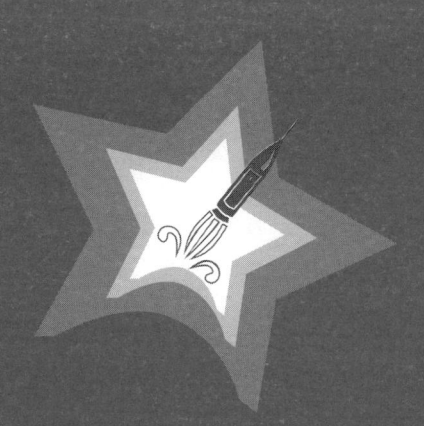

Reading

1 Read through the whole paper carefully, making sure you are clear what the booklet is about. Re-read sections you find confusing. Then read the questions a section at a time. The question booklet will make it very clear which questions are about which piece of text.

2 Check how many marks can be awarded as you read each question. (It will be in brackets at the side.) Many of the questions are 1 mark only, so don't spend loads of time on these. Use your time on the 2, 3 or 4 mark questions and **always refer to the text to support your answer**.

3 Work as fast as you can without being careless. If you have some time left at the end, go back and check your answers, starting with the higher mark ones.

4 Don't worry about answering in full sentences, unless you find that helpful. You won't get any marks for the sentences – the marks are for the content of your answers.

Spelling and handwriting

1 Apply spelling rules and think carefully. Does it look right? If you're not sure, try writing two options on the paper, but don't forget to cross out one of them!

2 Take your time with the handwriting – it's not a race! Any mistakes will be heavily penalised, so use your rubber if you have to. (But make sure you've got a new rubber that won't leave nasty blotches on the paper.)

Good luck!

The 2003 SATs

Key Facts

★ The Key Stage 2 National Tests (or SATs) take place in the middle of May in Year 6. You will be tested on Maths, English and Science.

★ The tests take place in your school and will be marked by examiners – not your teacher!

★ You will get your results in July, two months after you take the tests.

★ Most children will get a Level 4 or above with about 30% getting to Level 5 (though this varies in each subject).

★ Individual test scores are not made public but a school's combined scores are published in what are commonly known as league tables.

The English National Tests

You will take four tests in English. These are designed to test your Reading, Writing and Spelling. Your handwriting will be assessed through the Writing Tests.

The Writing Tests

There are now two Writing Tests – one short (about 20 minutes) and one longer test (about 45 minutes). Remember to keep your handwriting neat for these tests.

Where to go to get help

Pages 6 to 33 are designed to help you succeed in the Writing Tests and include information about writing fiction and non-fiction.

Pages 40 to 50 and pages 56 to 57 will help you to 'give voice to your writing', sharpen up your punctuation and improve your grammar.

Page 59 gives you advice on how to improve your handwriting, which is marked through the Writing Tests.

The Reading Test

There is one test to assess your reading comprehension. It will last about 1 hour. In this test you will be given a series of texts and an answer paper. You will be allowed to use the texts to answer the questions, so you won't need to memorise them.

Where to go to get help

Pages 34 to 39 give you advice on how to answer reading comprehension questions, which will help with the Reading Test.

The Spelling Test

There is one 15 minute Spelling Test. Your teacher will read a passage (or play a cassette with someone else reading the passage). You will have to write the words to complete the passage.

Where to go to get help

Pages 52 to 55 give you practice in spelling, including a list of key words to learn before your test.

Changes to the 2003 SATs

There are several changes you should be aware of in this year's SATs:

1) There is now one long and one short Writing Test (instead of two long ones).
2) There will be a new mark scheme for Writing.
3) Handwriting will only be assessed in the Writing Test – there is no separate handwriting test.

Index

A
active voice — 46, 47
adjectives — 48, 49
adventure stories — 25-28, 41
adverbs — 50
alliteration — 48
Almond, David — 44, 50
apostrophes — 55
apostrophes – omission — 55
apostrophes – possession — 55
argument — 18-20

B
balanced argument — 18-20

C
clause — 40, 42, 43
cliffhanger — 25, 27, 28
colon — 58
commas — 56
Compassion in World Farming — 38, 39
complex sentences — 40, 42, 43, 44
compound sentences — 40, 42
connectives — 7, 11, 17, 18, 21, 26
consonant — 54
Cross, Gillian — 44

D
dash — 58
Dickens, Charles — 51
discussion — 18

E
ellipsis — 58
emotional language — 18
explanation — 16-17

F
fairy tales — 32-33
fiction — 24-33, 45, 60-61
Fine, Anne — 36, 37
formal style — 8, 9, 10

G
grammar — 40-47

H
handwriting — 59, 61-63
How to use this book — 4-5

I
instructions and procedures — 11-12

K
key facts — 28, 34, 40, 45, 47, 51, 52
Key Stage 2 Tests — 60-63

L
long vowels — 54

M
metaphor — 51
myths and legends — 29-31

N
narrative — 13, 24, 33, 44, 45
non-chronological report — 8-10
non-fiction — 7-23, 45, 60-61
nouns — 48, 49

P
paragraphs — 45
passive voice — 46-47
pluralisation — 53
plurals — 53
practice questions — 7, 10, 12, 15, 17, 20, 23, 28, 31, 33, 35, 41, 42, 43, 44, 47, 49, 50, 53, 54, 55, 56, 58
punctuation — 56-58

R
reading comprehension — 34-39, 61
Reading Test — 61-63
recount — 13-15
repetition — 51
reports — 10, 13
results — 62

S
sentences — 40-44, 46, 47, 56
simile — 51
simple sentences — 40, 41, 42, 44
speech marks — 57
Spelling Test — 52, 59, 61-63
spelling — 51, 52-55, 61-63
subordinate clause — 40, 42, 43, 44

T
technical language — 8, 9, 16, 17, 18, 19
test technique — 60-61
time connectives — 7, 13, 15, 26, 30, 33

V
verbs — 50
vocabulary — 48-51

W
Westall, Robert — 40
writing fiction — 24-33, 45, 60-61
writing non-fiction — 6-23, 45, 60-61
Writing Test — 60-63